WORD
Energetics

WORD
Energetics

An Introductory Guide

Lorian Collins

To order additional copies of this book, contact:
Xlibris
1-888-795-4274
www.Xlibris.com
Orders@Xlibris.com
722327

Dedications

To Abraham, one of the most loving and powerful teachers in my life so far!

To Debra Koch who planted the seed for this book with her homemade framed version of my name as an acronym.

To my son Nicholas, who played the ABC gratitude game with me as a good night ritual.

To Betty, the first person to read and appreciate the original acronym for PEACE.

Introduction

The words contained herein are meant to uplift individually and collectively. Meditating upon them in whatever way is pleasing to you will be of benefit to us all. Words that affirm deserve attention and reverence. Experimenting with these and other words can be a wonderful conscious meditation which will always invite you to higher vibrations and responding life experiences.

Words that inspire call to be shared. You may want to experiment with the joyous ways you can incorporate these words and their accompanying energy into your thoughts and conversations throughout the day. Awareness of additional words that call to you may occur. Pay attention to these and their essence. What feelings do they invoke in you? An amazing new concept of word search awaits us, and it is most certainly good fun to look for words that feel pleasing! I like to make a playful game of it, searching for treasured high-flying words. It puts a refreshing new twist on the concept of word search. Do allow yourself to play with creating your own acronyms too.

Personally enhanced word experiences have come to me at stop lights, from license plates, and car and billboard signage. Since I'm a visual learner, my process is assisted by seeing the words and letters. Other may be auditorily oriented, so they may resonate more with words through song lyrics or conversations. Either way, words can and do have an influence in how we feel and the life experiences we create.

Acceptance of

Loving

Light-hearted

Opulent

Well-being

It's so pleasing to me that ALLOW is what I call my new happy verb! I love how fitting it is to richly begin this sourcebook with its delicious energy. Do you feel the difference between the words get and allow? I have one of my gifted therapists to thank for planting this seed several years ago. To get something can feel like hard work, angst, even control, whereas to allow feels open, easy and free.

I encourage you to treat your mind to this word gift today. You may use it as a mantra of sorts during your time of receptive listening, or you may read and contemplate the multi- layered acronym aloud to yourself for several minutes, or as long as it engages you. Find your pace as you will, and bask in the good vibrations it brings to you. Now just for fun, experiment with allowing it into your conversations and interactions as you go about your day.

Being

Empowered by

Love

Inspiration

Energy and

Focus

In both Religion and Spirituality, belief seems foundational. Yet how much time and energy do we put into beliefs that are other than uplifting and inspiring? With some nurturance, our beliefs can be like our solid and supportive friends.

By beginning with the word itself, as allowed here, perhaps we can begin to nourish the beliefs which truly reflect what we value and desire to live in our personal daily faith walks. By meditating individually on these words within the word (BEING, EMPOWERMENT, LOVE, INSPIRATION, ENERGY and FOCUS), you will allow yourself new insights. Following your quiet time with these, you may choose to move your experience to visual and kinesthetic levels, and write what beliefs you have that relate and resonate with each word. Pay close attention to how these feel. If you are pleased with your beliefs (friends), keep them and honor them, love them and live with them.

Celebrating

Readiness to

Express

Amazing and

Timely

Energy

Creative feels so expansive, flowing and fun! For me, creativity seems to be all about energy moving through us in a myriad of forms, longing for expression. Expression opportunities are limitless and seem to add their own joy and momentum to this word. Certainly, the energy and vibrations of this word are at the heart of this published work.

If you are inspired to add art to your book, do so, otherwise, take a large index card and write the word(s) on it. From a selection of several colored felt pens, choose your very favorite color (highlighters are best). Highlight the initial word, CREATE, and allow your energy to lead you into coloring/doodling/drawing however and whatever it wants to. Freedom and joy are calling you. Do you want to play?

Delicious

Entertainment of

Loving

Inspiring

Guided and

Happy

Thoughts

Delight, delighted, delightful; I love sprinkling my sentences with these delicious delicacies in any form! How about a little word play here; DELIGHTFUL spelled backwards is fulighted! May we all be infused with full light this day. I have also noted that when delight and appreciation hold hands, which they nearly always do, we begin to joyously vibrate with majorly expanded collaborative energy. We surely come to comprehend what inspired Brian Wilson of the Beach Boys, as he composed his hit song "Good Vibrations". More recently, you may have been blessed by the delightful vibrations of Pharrell William's song "Happy". This soaring song has entertained, loved, inspired and guided us and will continue to do so for decades to come. I can rarely hear this tune, (which is now in book form) without my body wanting to join in with a happy dance! I so appreciate Pharrell for sharing his gifts with us. Treat yourself to this tune at least once today!

Energy

Assisting

Serene

Efficiency

This is, by far, one of my favorite feeling words in this book, my vocabulary and my consciousness. Many of my days include walking and working meditations with this at their core. I commit myself to living EASE these days. My friends hear me speak of ease often, as I look, feel for, and invite it in. It pleases me immensely, that with practice, I have come to be quite familiar with energy assisting me with serene efficiency!

In 2009, as I began nursing my way through the wounds of divorce, I was reading a book by Esther and Jerry Hicks. I will never forget the feeling I had when I read the suggestion that life was meant to be fun and to feel good. This rather foreign idea was a spark of hope that resonated within me, and has since transformed into a long and luscious dance with ease as my partner. Care to dance?

Fun and
Relaxed with
Easy
Effervescence

I feel FREE as a rush of pleasing, positive, exhilarating energy! Perhaps this is because it connects me with my inner kid who was, at times, freer than the grown-up me of today. Certainly I felt easier at play, which was a natural daily pleasure then. An ongoing commitment now, is to do something fun/joyful for myself every day. The more I do this, the freer I feel!

What do you see and feel when you read this acronym? What areas of your life do you feel FREE in? Do you think and speak of these, making a point of celebrating this energy with others? Ever wonder how you can create more of this (feeling of free) for yourself?

Gifts

Revealed

Anytime we

Cease

Effort

It was a gift to receive a special delivery from this energetic bundle. The words seemed to call for some unique placement, so as to stand out from the others. Turns out they wanted to move, to dance across this page! I was delighted to listen and respond. Well, after all, I am talking and writing, and you, in this moment, are thinking and reading about GRACE here. It really offers quite a celebratory vibration, doesn't it? It is important to note that ceasing effort is a central key to our receptivity. A relaxed and open state allows for the most abundant flow of gifts.

My early Christian foundation regarding the grace of God comes to mind also. Recently, a friend of faith lovingly reminded me that God's grace is indeed sufficient. That being said, God's gifts could readily be adapted as the top two to initiate this magnificent grouping.

H O P E

H	O	P	E
a	p	u	n
p	t	r	g
p	i	p	a
i	o	o	g
e	n	s	e
r	s	e	d
		l	
		y	

I love being a participant in support groups and caring, conscious communities whenever and wherever I choose. One peer support group I belong to has adopted a saying that states, "Hope Lives Here". I'm reminded of this lovely affirmation as I feel and think on this word now. There have certainly been periods in my life devoid of hope. At these challenging points, I've seen myself request to borrow this precious thought/feeling commodity from others. I simply find others shining with the light of hope, state where I am, (seeking my lost hope), and ask that they share about their personal hope experiences. It is important to select people who are clearly in a state of high hope now, and willing to share their wealth with you. They will help you engage with happier options since they currently have access to them.

Further accomplishments of HOPE have been supported by consistently centering myself around people, places and things that inspire and uplift me. The more clearly and completely I commit to this, the more I resonate with the truth that, like the movie title, HOPE does indeed float!

There are a happy host of feel good words starting with the letter H. I invite you to look for, ponder on, and speak as many of them as you can today.

Incoming

New

Sources of

Power

Insight

Refreshment and

Exhilaration

Think on how fun it is to allow something new into your life; a home, car, relationship, or even a piece of clothing. There can be joyous enthusiasm all along the search, preparation, allowance and purchase phases. This acronym invites us to ponder on the fresh perspectives coming in to uplift us all. Shared inspirations can have the pebble in the pond effect, where the thought, message or action is gifted and then the ripple of energy expands out from the original center point. The amazing Art (Symbala) on the front of this book is a visual representation of this idea as well.

As you meditate on all or any of these words that please, explore with enhancing your experience by looking at the Symbala. Remember to share your inspirations......

Jubilant

Open

You (Me)

I have a very special kinship with this word, as my middle name is Joye. Thank you Marian, (Mom) for your creative gifts of both my first and my middle name.

You may have noticed children live in Joy, a lot! Maybe we can catch it from them. You know, like instead of catching a cold or flu, JOY could be spread. Indeed, what a more wonderful world it will be as we all become carriers. One way to begin is to let these brilliant beings (children) be our natural teachers, and we, in turn can be their open, willing and receptive students. Let's see, I think I will register for Just for Fun 101, or Living a Laughter-Driven Life!

Noting the you/me interchange here reminds us that we are certainly all in this together. Is there any better way to be together than in the magnificence of shared Joy? I will complete this page with how I often close letters, texts and conversations; Joy to Us!

Kindly

Interactions

Nicely

Delivered with

Respect to

Everyone

Dear to us

I love that this word has kind at the front. Kindness packs power like nothing else. A related word gift that became one of my favorite bumper stickers was "Practice Random Acts of Kindness". In turn, kind begins with kin, which often refers to family. I like to think of my family as worldwide, which provides vast opportunities for me to spread the loving energy that emerges here. A personal note is that I've often found it easier to share this with my universal family than my family of origin. Others will experience quite the opposite. Either way, we are all winners as we experiment with KINDRED in our daily lives. Choosing to have this at the heart of all our interactions will produce a momentum of reciprocal appreciation that will be quite pleasing indeed!

Luminous

Open

Vibrant

Energy

This is another of my favorites. I like reading this over and over, either to myself or aloud. Basking here is strongly suggested, as it feels soooo good. I also like pairing any of these two and letting them move through my consciousness with their loving vibration. Have you noticed how many of the acronyms herein contain the word energy? Energy abounds through all these gifted words (thus the writing of this little book), while some seem to call for the extra nod, as LOVE does here.

Open is at the heart and soul of this acronym, gently reminding us that LOVE is about an energetic exchange or flow, and is most joyously experienced with our incoming and outgoing channels open wide. In regard to this, I have learned the importance of nurturing a balance of giving and receiving. Yes, I surely do enjoy remembering to take turns being the lover and the loved one. It is so much more fun this way! Try it, you'll like it.

Miracles

Abundantly

Gifting

Insight and

Clarity

Throughout the years, I have been wowed by the MAGIC of the entertainers whom I watch with wonder as they perform their tricks. Their stage accomplishments seem to me, miraculous at times. What we, as the audience, are often unaware of, is how much attention, practice and focus goes behind these smooth, yet dazzling performances. So I'm not proposing practice of magic tricks here, but certainly familiarizing ourselves with some of the components contained herein; Miracles, Abundant gifting (to and from), Insight and Clarity. Do this and watch for your ideas and experience of MAGIC to expand!

A wise mentor told me years ago that miracles are natural, and I recall hearing about a book entitled, Everyday Miracles. My response to these natural, daily occurrences of miracles is an encouraging and enthusiastic, Why not? Here's another worthy query to ponder; Would we rather believe what we see, or see what we believe?

Newly

Observant with

Wonder.

There is much emphasis and a great deal of support for the experience and practice of being present (in the now). Books, meditations, and aspects of some religions are avenues through which this has most often revealed itself.

It is my pleasure to feature NOW in its enhanced acronymic form for us to go deeper with! On a large index card write the word and accompanying acronym and refer to it often as you are out and about today. Appreciate how many times you can tap into and feel the richness as you remind yourself into this "living meditation" by being Newly Observant with Wonder! In our thoughts, words and deeds, let's go for it and get all our senses involved in this vibrational vastness!

Be sure to share your marvelous findings with another fortunate person.....

Opulent

Possibilities

Endless in

Nature

This feels like a rush of joyous buoyant energy with a very high and fine vibration offering loving caresses for our body, mind and spirits! Opulent brings to mind diamonds, (a pocketful, as a matter of fact). Did you know that endless possibilities have been around a long time and will continue to be? Nature can have two meanings here. It is interesting how my being out in nature puts me into my most open stances. I find my practice of a state of being open is a key to my receptivity, and allowing myself more of what I want.

As you meditate on this word and accompanying words, you may notice images coming to you, or you may be aware of a more somatic response with shifts and various sensations in your body. May our new-found places of openness bless us, and indeed they will! Merry Openings to us all and to all a good life!

Precious

Energy

Always

Creating

Ease

Being a peace-seeker nearly all of my life, it is no surprise that this was the first word combination to be revealed to me. One of my favorite church service traditions is looking into the eyes of other congregants and exchanging the loving message of "Peace be with you" with the accompanying response, "and also with you". What a loving opportunity this is with our selves and others, and to truly be present for these interactions is an honor indeed.

A ceramic garden sign in a large cedar pot on my deck reads PEACE, and since I meditate on my deck nearly all year round, I have ample opportunity to see and be and feel this daily. What if we refreshed our perspective on living to include peace and ease as our focus? I often enjoy lovingly reminding myself to choose ease throughout my daily decision making processes. Ease is good.

Quintessential

Uplifting

Into

Exceptional

Thoughts

More and more, quiet places beckon me as I am soothed by the stillness. I am eternally appreciative for retreat centers that provide opportunities for us to be silent, some including no cell phone service! As a business owner, this is a precious gift to be totally "unplugged" since the restorative power in these respites is quite substantial. On a smaller scale, moments of solitude can be cultivated daily in our meditation times, nature walks, or even driving in the car. When was the last time you chose to leave radio or music off while in your car?

If we are accustomed to living on stimuli overload, it can be challenging to be quiet with ourselves or others. In the early 90's, I was blessed to attend a silent weekend retreat lead by Thich Naht Hanh. During this time, I found myself compelled to leave and go converse with talking folks in the nearby town of Rhinebeck. Over the years, I have acquired a definite craving for the sweet serenity that comes in silence. Instead of running from this, I now run to the quiet spaces, as it seems that my fullness presents itself most freely during these times. I remember how thrilled I was when my son and I were visiting a center in Oregon and he surprised me by choosing to share sacred space in the silent hot tub. This experience was so pleasing, we designated one night a week for suppers without words. Try coming home to your precious self by allowing just a little more time in stillness today....

Respite and

Encouragement

Leading to

Inspiration

Energy and

Freedom

Respite denotes a break, so why not give ourselves one (or many) as we choose healthy distractions (thoughts and activities) which assist us in feeling a little better and freer. Encouragement feels like one of the greatest gifts I can give myself and my loved ones.

If we are experiencing physical pain or major grief, we are usually motivated toward getting some relief. What about allowing this concept to provide broader benefits for us? Just for fun, let's see if we can consciously seek comfort from minor irritations, or worrisome thoughts as they begin to arise. I initiate this change by interrupting and redirecting my negative thinking, and replacing it with something I feel good about. I am honestly astounded at the number of daily opportunities I have to change the direction of my thoughts!

Can you see and feel the flow of energy and how these words build on each other as you read down the page? Here's a magnificent, yet simple math problem; Encouragement plus Inspiration equals Energy and Freedom.

Sensuous

Open

Uplifting

Leading to a

Full

Understanding of

Love

Once again my mind goes to music as I contemplate this scrumptious word. Lena Horne and Ella Fitzgerald were two gifted singers who shared their soulfulness with us. Many other musical artists have assisted in connecting us with our own sweet spirits. Even now, the memory of my favorite voices and songs raises my vibration. That is how it works; hear it, think it, feel it, speak it (sing it), and we bring ourselves there for a more inspired, elevated and loving experience.

Are you open for a higher understanding of your "soul self"? Who are some of your cherished musicians? Have you treated yourself to a listen lately? I find this continues to be a very rich and rewarding journey that leads me into other forms of Soul-filled Art. Additional worthy personal queries are; What touches you at a soul level? How do you connect with your soulful self? What does it feel like? Meditating on this word grouping may introduce you to some new awareness. Common indicators for me of feeling soulful are gentle tears of awe gracing my cheeks, or what Abraham calls "thrill bumps" (goose bumps) dancing up and down my arms.

Truths

Spiritual

Underlying

Reliance on

Total

Since these words are calling us to higher experiences of energy and thought, it is fitting to have them placed on the page in this stair step, upward movement configuration. This acronym will serve us the most if we are clear on just what our Spiritual Truths are. I find these truths reside in our core as Love, Peace, Freedom, Joy and Oneness. It requires trust to begin to live more from this precious place within, and it also generates more trust as we do so.

Of all the words on these pages, TRUST requires the most practice for me personally. Discernment of what and who I may trust has been a lengthy and dedicated journey. It began with commitment to a relationship with myself; to discover and consciously connect with the love, joy and tender peace inside of me.

Ultimate

Provision of

Love

Inspired

Freedom of

Thought

How would the course of our days change if we were to focus consistently upon uplifting and being uplifted? Jerry Hicks, co-author of several best-selling books, often spoke of desiring that his interactions result in all parties involved feeling better afterward. Conscious intention of this has inspired many more meaningful connections in my life.

We are called again to a balance in the giving and receiving of the precious gifts we share, and it's so important to recognize that who we are is the most precious gift of all! Have you ever been invited to a party where the host declines material gifts, adding sweetly that you and your presence are the gift? I just love being on both ends of these types of uplifting conversations.

UPLIFT is a favorite meditation for me. It is wonderful to allow it to infuse its energy throughout my daily affairs. Are your thoughts fueled by love and freedom? Can you imagine this and what feelings, they may in turn produce? This combination is high soaring; your conscious contemplation here will most certainly be uplifting!

Vibrating with

Intentional

Beauty while

Resonating with

Amazing

New

Treasures

As I meditate on this for the day, I can watch for that which is beautiful and treasured to enter into my experiences. I love the word resonate, especially if I'm in a centered place; it indicates that more of what I am thinking and feeling about is on its way to me! The Law of Attraction has been written about in many books before this one. This V word oozes this law..... What do you wish to create for yourself today? It is our choice, our responsibility, indeed our honor to imagine treasures we desire. As a kid, I always enjoyed the Easter egg hunts, recalling that the hunt was as fun as the find. I'm inviting us all to a very extraordinary treasure hunt personalized with all that delights us. Yippeeeeeee!!!

Wide

Open to the

New

Delivery of

Ecstatic

Reminders

Wonder is such an amazing state. I usually get there easily when out in nature or connecting with the animals I work, live and play with. Another wonder avenue is travel. One of the reasons that I love travel is that it takes me to unfamiliar places, provides refreshing interactive options with people, and propels me fundamentally toward a sense of adventure which is always a" feel good" for me. A place of curiosity, combined with receptivity that can bring me to heightened levels of profound discovery is certainly worthy of my commitment.

Now it's your turn. When did you last feel a sense of wonder? Did you know that children are in this place most of the time? Once again, it might behoove us to turn to some of our master teachers who have not yet experienced the loss of this. Not that your place of WONDER will be the same path as a child you observe, but it may be a helpful part of your process in mapping out your own journey.

eXquisite

Awakenings to

New

Amazing and

Deliberate

Understanding

O.K., I do admit to being curious, in the earlier stages of this manuscript, as to how the X word was going to play out and present itself. As you can see, some creative license was exercised.

Let's go! Let's go in our mind and with our words and in our lives to what the dictionary defines as a place of great beauty, luxury and contentment. Have you ever experienced a delicious guided meditation that was rich and pleasing to all your senses? These are the type with a soothing soft-spoken narrator describing a precious place to see and feel yourself. These meditations are specifically created for a peaceful and pleasing experience in body, mind and spirit. This word calls us to live this caliber of meditation experience. We can do this! I have and do live this. It really is an extraordinary opportunity. Pay attention to your personalized XANADUS. What paths (choices) are pleasing and beautiful and brilliant to you? This is especially for you (me). Our XANADUS await!

You are

Ease and

Sureness

Think about the last time you responded with an enthusiastic YES to an invitation that thrilled you. You were probably definite, clear and joyous at the thought of doing what activity was involved, or who it would have you sharing with. There was also likely no hesitation before your answer. It is my desire to live a life where I say yes more from this exuberance, and an equally authentic NO, when inspiration is absent for me within the opportunity.

Can you feel the high-flying energy of this clear and concise word group? I can; it makes me want to cheer yeses to myself/ourselves, our lives, and others who are doing the same. When we ask for help and it comes, may we say a resounding yes to it. If we want more money, and it comes, may we be quick and sure to receive it. If love is what we long for and comes calling, may we open our hearts and welcome it in with our loving embrace.

Zesty

Effervescent

Streams of

Thought

Full of

Unconditional

Love

What comes to mind is a cornucopia of pleasure here. Imagine a sensational taste or exotic flavor upon our tongue, a hot tub jetting swarms of warm soothing bubbles aimed to please our muscles, and a fullness of the kind of love without longing that God does best, yet we all have the capacity for and can tap into when we intentionally choose. The pairing of POSITIVE THOUGHT and UNCONDITIONAL LOVE creates an energy that will certainly lift us to a higher plain. Rita Coolidge gifted us her perspective on this as she sang the popular 70's song, "Your Love is Lifting Me Higher".

Notice that THOUGHT is at the center of this word, not just one, but streams of it. Several positive powerful streams of thought do produce a current of golden opportunities. Yes indeed, there is gold in these here streams; may we make up our minds to mine for it with our sight, our thought, our activity, and our voice.

I would be delighted to hear about your expanded and inspiring word experiences. Feel free to share via my email at; WordEnergetics@gmail.com, or Facebook at; Lorian Collins - Word Energertics